The Alphabet Book of Verses:

Teaching a child to know and love God and His Word

ISBN 978-0-692-95478-2

Words by Kimmie Jacobs
Graphic Design by Chris Harrell
Illustrations by Jo Kosobucki

Printed in China 2017.

Dear Parents,

ears ago when our first daughter was just learning to talk, God impressed on my heart the importance of teaching her to love and memorize His Word. A friend had a little booklet with a verse for each letter of the alphabet. I thought, "I could make something like that!" So I spent several weeks pouring over scripture and thinking through what verses would be best to instill in a young toddler's mind. I wanted verses that communicated the gospel as well as verses that addressed issues a toddler/preschooler could grasp. After choosing the verses, I bought several coloring books (since I am definitely NOT an artist!) and colored pictures to go with each verse. I assembled the book on pieces of poster board and had it bound and laminated. My husband and I used that verse book with each of our 5 children. My husband challenged me to publish the book so I could share it with others. Well, weeks turned into months then into years. We got caught up in the busyness of raising 5 children and, before we knew it, that sweet little girl who motivated me to create the verse book grew up and got married! Now with the thought of grandchildren on the horizon, my motivation was renewed to find a real illustrator for the book and try to publish it. God led me to Jo Kosobucki who has such a beautiful gift with watercolors, but more importantly, shares my passion to instill God's Word in children's hearts.

I cannot stress enough the importance of God's Word in our lives! II Timothy 3:16 says that "All scripture is inspired by God and profitable for teaching, for reproof, for correction, for training in righteousness; so that the man of God may be adequate, equipped for every good work." It is imperative, as sons and daughters of the King, that you teach your children to know, love, and handle accurately the Word of God (II Tim. 2:15). Deuteronomy 6:6-9 says to write the words of God on our hearts, to teach our children the Word at every opportunity. It is my prayer that this book will be a tool to help you teach your child to treasure God's Word and hide it in his heart. **Please take time to read the "How to Use this Book" on the facing page to the right so you can get the maximum experience for you and your child.**

How to Use This Book:

As with any alphabet book, each letter of the alphabet has a word to help a child learn his letters and sounds. However, unlike other ABC books, learning letters and sounds is secondary to the goal of teaching a toddler to memorize God's Word. Each page has a corresponding mini lesson to give you ideas for teaching the concept in the verse. These mini lessons are just suggestions to get your creative juices flowing as you disciple your child. The passages have been color coded. The focal word is in *color bold italics*. Some of the passages are longer and may be too long for a young toddler to learn. So the abbreviated passage is in **bold italic**. The **light italic** words can be memorized later as a child ages and grows in his memorization skills. It is often easier to memorize something when you make a song out of it. For that reason I highly recommend purchasing Steve Green's "Hide 'Em In Your Heart" CD's. You will find songs to many of the verses in this book on volumes 1 and 2 and also the "Hide 'Em In Your Heart: Praise and Worship" CD. I also encourage you to be creative and make up your own songs to go with the verses!

Psalm 56:3-4 NIV

•

When I am afraid, I will trust in you. *In God, whose word I praise, in God I trust; I will not be afraid. What can mortal man do to me?*

A is for Afraid

Psalm 56:3-4 NIV

•

When I am afraid, I will trust in you. *In God, whose word I praise, in God I trust; I will not be afraid. What can mortal man do to me?*

Parent Help:

What are you afraid of? Is thunder scary? Are there animals you're scared of? What is the little girl in the picture afraid of? What do you do when you are afraid? Who helps you? What if Mommy and Daddy aren't around to help? This verse tells us there is someone who can always help us. Who is that? *(God)* Does God ever leave us? Is there anything stronger than God? So when we are afraid we can trust God to protect us. He will never leave us, and nothing is more powerful than God!

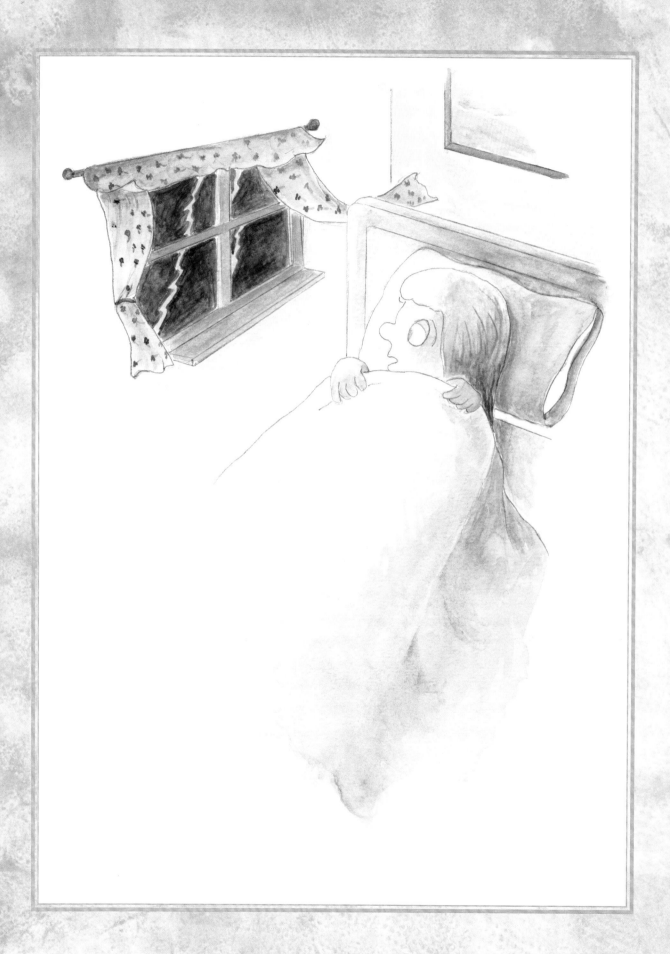

B is for Believe

Acts 16:31 NIV

•

They replied, **"Believe** *in the Lord Jesus, and you* **will be saved** *— you and your household."*

Parent Help:

Who are we to believe in? *(Jesus)* What did he do for us? *(He saved us)* What did he save us from? *(eternal death)* How did he do that? *(He died on the cross and took the punishment for all our sin.)* What do we need to do to be saved? *(believe in Jesus!)* How does the little girl in the picture look? *(happy)* The Bible tells us that if we abide in Christ our joy will be full. In His presence is the fullness of joy!

C is for Children

Ephesians 6:1 NIV

•

Children, obey your parents in the Lord,

for this is right.

Parent Help:

Who does God tell you to obey? *(your parents)* Why? *(it is right)* Is it sometimes hard to obey? When? What happens when you disobey? God commands children to obey their parents for their protection. Your parents love you and want what is best for you. It's their job to protect and care for you and it's your job to obey them. When you obey your parents you are obeying God too!

D is for Do

Philippians 2:14   NIV

•

Do ***everything without complaining or arguing,***

Parent Help:

What does this verse tell us? *(don't complain or argue)* What things should we do without complaining or arguing? *(everything)* What do you complain about? Do you ever argue with your brother or sister? Doing everything without complaining or arguing is hard to do! Who can help us with that? *(Jesus)* The next verse in Philippians 2 gives us the reason why we should not complain or argue. It tells us that we will become blameless and pure and others will see the light of Jesus in us and know that we are children of God. We are actually shining our light for Jesus when we choose not to complain or argue!

E is for Encourage

I Thessalonians 5:11 NIV

·

Therefore encourage one another and build each other up, just as in fact you are doing.

Parent Help:

What does "encourage" mean? *(to say kind words to someone in order to make them feel better)* If your brother or sister fell and broke their toy or skateboard like the boy in the picture, what are some ways you could encourage them? How do we sometimes use words to discourage people? When we are encouraging people it's like we are building up a tall tower with blocks. It makes people happy. When we use mean words and discourage people it's like knocking down someone's tower of blocks. It makes them sad. Let's choose to build people up, not tear them down.

F is for Fall

Romans 3:23 NIV

For all have sinned and fall short of the glory of God.

Parent Help:

Who has sinned? *(all people)* What is sin? *(anything that breaks God's commands.)* What sin did the boy in the picture do? *(he intentionally broke his brother's lego building)* The Bible tells us that God is holy. That means that He is perfect and never sins. He is full of glory. Because God is holy, He can't be in the presence of sin, so there can't be any sin in heaven. Since we sin, we fall short.

Trying to do good things to get to heaven is like trying to throw a ball to Grandma's house. We can never do it. We fall short. *(Try taking the child outside to show the impossibility of this feat)* We need a Savior. We need Jesus. He paid the price for our sin when He died on the cross. When we believe in Him we are saved from the punishment for our sin and given eternal life.

G is for Giver

II Corinthians 9:7 NIV

•

Each man should give what he has decided in his heart to give, not reluctantly or under compulsion, ***for God loves a cheerful*** *giver.*

Parent Help:

What kind of giver does God love? *(a cheerful giver)* What are some things we can give to God? *(money, time, ourselves)* What could you give to God today? *(you could share your toys with others with a happy heart...brainstorm other ideas)* The first part of the verse tells us God doesn't want us to give because we think we have to, or reluctantly. He wants us to give with a happy, cheerful heart.

H is for Heart

Psalm 119:11 NIV

·

I have hidden your word in my heart

that I might not sin against you.

Parent Help:

Do you know what your heart is? Can you point to it? The word for heart here does not mean the organ that pumps blood through your body. It refers to your inner man, your will or your mind. What does the psalmist say he hid in his heart? *(God's Word)* Why does he hide God's Word in his heart? *(so he won't sin)* Hide means to treasure or to memorize. Memorizing God's Word will protect us from sin. Ephesians tells us that God's Word is like a sword. We can use it to fight off Satan who tempts us to sin.

I is for In

Genesis 1:1 NIV

·

In the beginning God created the heavens and the earth.

Parent Help:

Who created the world? *(God)* **(Take time to read Genesis chapter 1 together.)** Who existed before anything else was made? *(God)* How did God make the world? *(He spoke)* Can you make something by just speaking? Only God can make something from nothing. What are some of the things God made?

J is for Joyful

Proverbs 17:22 NASB

•

A joyful heart is good medicine,

but a broken spirit dries up the bones.

Parent Help:

Do you like to take medicine? Sometimes medicine tastes very yucky! Why do we take medicine? *(to help us get better)* What does this verse say is good medicine? *(a joyful heart)* How can we have a joyful heart? *(we choose to be happy even when something bad happens)* What happened to the little girl in the picture? *(she broke her foot)* Is she grumpy because she has to be in the hospital? No, she's choosing to be joyful, despite her hard circumstances. Do you like to be around sad and angry people? No! It makes you feel sad and angry too. When we choose to be joyful it not only helps us feel better, it helps other people feel better too!

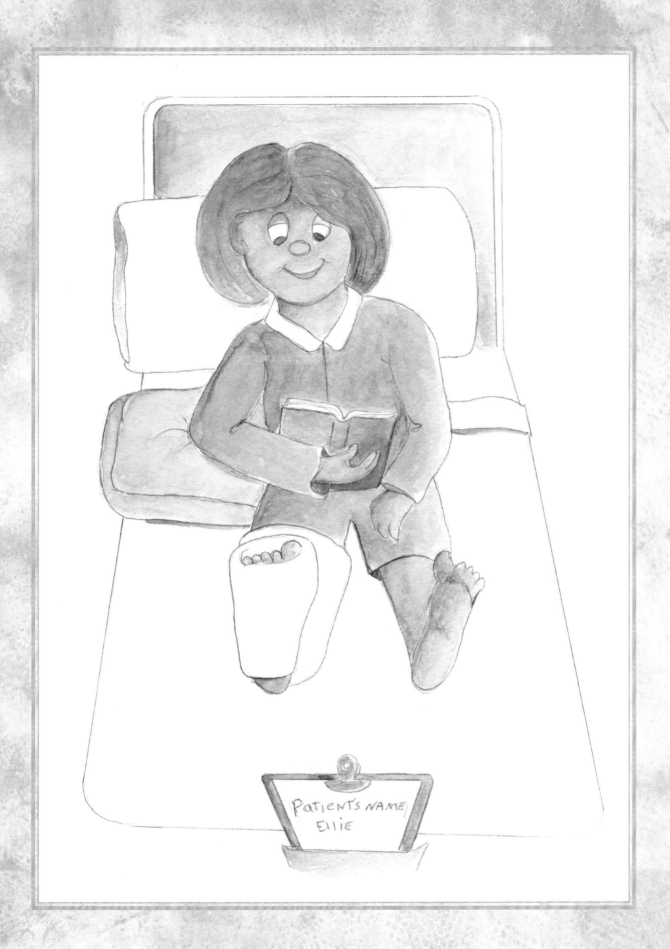

K is for Keep

Psalm 34:13 NIV

•

Keep your tongue from evil and

your lips from speaking lies.

Parent Help:

What does God command here? *(don't speak evil things or lies)* How can we speak evil? *(say unkind words to someone, call them names...)* What is a lie? *(speaking something that is not true)* What is the boy lying about in the picture? *(he's saying he didn't break the window)* God tells us to use our mouths to speak kindness and truth, not evil and lies.

L is for Love

•

Jesus replied: **"'Love the Lord your God with all your heart and with all your soul and with all your mind.'**

Parent Help:

Who are we supposed to love? *(God)* With what? *(all our heart, soul, and mind)* God commands us to love Him with every part of us. How do we demonstrate our love for God? I John 5:3 tells us that we will show we love God by obeying His commands. If we love God we will do what He tells us to do in the Bible. The Bible also tells us that we show our love for God by loving people. If we say we love God, but hate our brother, the Bible says we are a liar. *(I John 4:20)* How is the girl in the picture demonstrating her love for God? *(she's reading the Bible)* We also show that we love God by spending time with Him reading the Bible and praying.

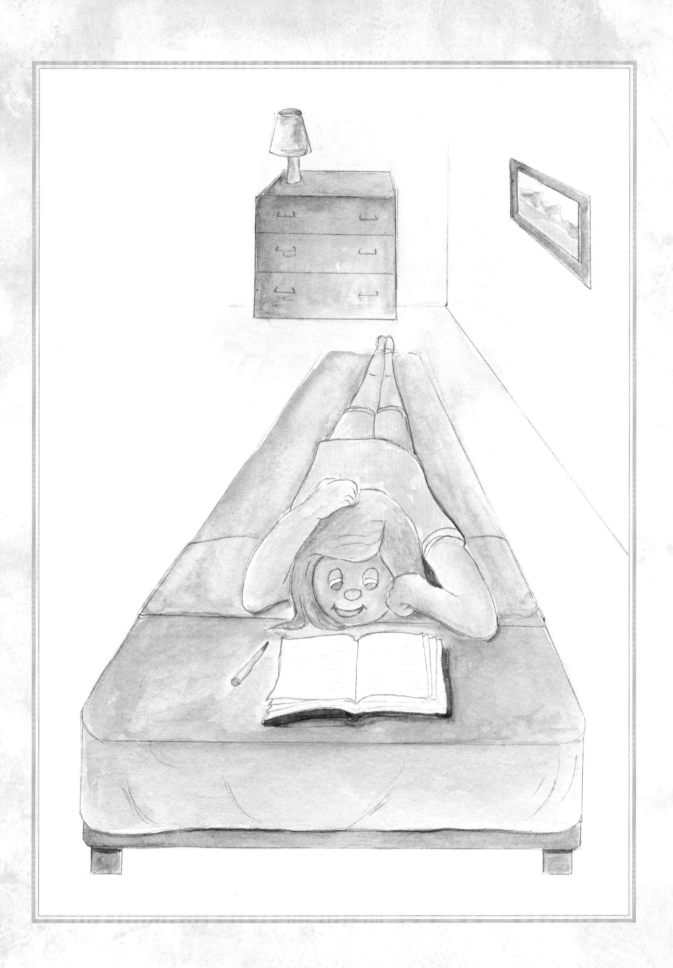

M is for Mouth

Psalm 19:14 NIV

•

May the words of my mouth ***and the meditation***

of my heart be pleasing in your sight,

O LORD, my Rock and my Redeemer.

Parent Help:

This is a prayer of David. He is asking God to help him with two things. First, he asks God to help the words of his mouth to be pleasing to God. How can we speak words that please God? *(speak kind words to others, praise God with songs, show contentment...)* How are the children in the picture using their words to please God? *(they are singing praises to Him)* Second, he asks God to help the meditations of his heart to be pleasing to God. What does meditation mean? *(to think about something)* So David wants his words and his thoughts to please God. He doesn't just want to speak pure words. He want to think good thoughts.

N is for Neighbor

Matthew 22:39 NIV

•

And the second is like it:

*'Love your **neighbor** as yourself.'*

Parent Help:

Who are we to love? *(our neighbor)* Who is your neighbor? It's not just the people who live on your street. In the Bible a man once asked Jesus, "Who is my neighbor?" Jesus told him a story about a good Samaritan man who showed love and kindness to even his enemy. Jesus told the man to do the same. **(You may want to read the story of the Good Samaritan, Luke 10:25-37)** So our neighbors are all the people we meet, even the ones who aren't kind to us. How is the boy in the picture showing love for his neighbor? *(he's helping a woman who is blind bring in her groceries)* How can you show love to your neighbor today?

O is for Overcome

Romans 12:21 NIV

•

Do not be **overcome** *by evil,*

but **overcome** *evil with good.*

When someone is mean to you how does that make you feel? How do you want to treat them? *(usually we want to get even)* What does the Bible tell us to do when people are mean to us? *(show kindness to them)* Jesus gave us an example to follow in this. The soldiers and religious leaders and Jewish people were all very cruel to him. But He continued to show kindness and patience. He showed His love for them and for us by dying on the cross to take our punishment for sin. Romans 5:8 says, that "while we were still sinners, Christ died for us." When we ask Jesus to be our Savior, the Holy Spirit comes to live in us and gives us the power to be kind to those who are unkind to us.

P is for Peace

Colossians 3:15 NIV

•

Let the **peace** *of Christ rule in your hearts,*

since as members of one body you were

called to **peace**. *And be thankful.*

Parent Help:

Peace is having a calm spirit. It's choosing to have a happy, contented heart even in situations you don't like. For parents it might look like being calm in a traffic jam or not getting angry when your son breaks your favorite bowl. For children it might look like not throwing a fit when it's time to leave the playground and go home. How are the boys in the picture letting the peace of Christ rule in their hearts? *(they are being good sports at the end of the game)* What does peace look like for you? One way to demonstrate a peaceful heart is to have a thankful attitude. How can we be thankful even in bad circumstances? Only with the help of the Holy Spirit.

Q is for Quarrel

Proverbs 15:18 NIV

•

A hot-tempered man stirs up dissension, but

a patient man calms a *quarrel*.

What is a quarrel? *(an argument)* That big word "dissension" also means to argue or fight. Do you ever argue with your brothers or sisters? Or your friends? Does God want us to quarrel? Remember the previous verse for letter "P"? What does God tell us should rule our hearts in Colossians 3:15?

(peace) Can you remember the verse for letter "D"? *(see if they can recite Philippians 2:14)* Philippians 2:14 says that when we choose not to argue or complain we shine as bright lights for Jesus. So let's be patient and calm the quarrels before they start!

R is for Rejoice

•

***Rejoice** in the Lord always.*

*I will say it again: **Rejoice**!*

Parent Help:

What does rejoice mean? *(be happy and full of joy)* What does it mean to rejoice in the Lord? *(praise God, thank Him)* When should we rejoice? *(always)* Should we praise Jesus only when good things happen? What about when bad things happen? Does Jesus want us to praise Him then? Yes! He wants us to praise Him and rejoice all the time! Paul, the writer of this verse, didn't just tell us one time to rejoice...He said it twice! When something is repeated in the Bible it means it's important. The writer really wants you to get the message. So don't just rejoice on the good days. Rejoice every day!

S is for Spirit

Galatians 5:22,23 NIV

•

But the fruit of the **Spirit** *is love, joy, peace, patience, kindness, goodness, faithfulness, gentleness, and* **self-control.** *Against such things there is no law.*

Parent Help:

Do you know that when you ask Jesus to be your Savior He sends His Holy Spirit to come live inside of you? As we read the Bible and pray the Holy Spirit produces fruit in our life! Not fruit we can eat like apples and bananas! But the fruit of good deeds. The Holy Spirit teaches us how to love others, how to be kind, how to be patient, and how to control our anger. These are qualities that only the Spirit can build in us. And the Bible tells us there are no laws against these qualities! We always need more of this kind of fruit!

T is for Trust

Proverbs 3:5 NIV

•

Trust in the LORD with all your heart and

lean not on your own understanding;

Parent Help:

What does it mean to trust? *(to believe someone will do what they say they will do)* The picture gives us a good visual of trust. The little girl is trusting her dad to make sure she doesn't fall. She is putting her entire weight on the bike and trusting her Dad to hold on until she's balanced. When we trust God it's like putting our whole weight on Him and believing that He will protect us and do what is best for us. We don't always understand why God allows some things to happen in our lives. But we can't trust our understanding. God is the only one who is worthy of and strong enough to handle our trust. He will always do what will bring Him glory and bring us good.

U is for Unity

Psalm 133:1 NIV

•

*How good and pleasant it is when brothers live together in **unity**!*

Parent Help:

Unity means "as one." It means getting along, not arguing or fighting. This verse says it's good and pleasant when brothers live in unity. When people are kind to each other and get along with each other it's pleasant to be around them. Have you ever been around people who are arguing or fighting? How does that make you feel? God wants those who love Him to show love for one another — to live in unity. When we do, we prove to others that we are His children.

V is for Vine

John 15:5 NIV

•

I am the **vine***; you are the branches.*

If a man remains in me and I in him, he will bear

much fruit; apart from me you can do nothing.

Parent Help:

In this verse Jesus is speaking and what does He call Himself? *(the vine)* The vine, as you see in the picture, is the main part of the plant. It's the part that provides the nourishment for the branches. Jesus calls us the branches. What would happen to the branches if they weren't connected to the vine?

(they would dry up and die) Could they bear fruit? *(no)* In the same way, if we don't stay connected to Jesus by reading the Bible, we can't bear the fruit of the Spirit. We can't do anything for God if we aren't connected to the Vine.

W is for Worship

•

Come, let us bow down in worship, let us kneel before the LORD our Maker.

Parent Help:

What do you think of when you hear the word worship? Worship means to praise God. To honor Him and give glory to Him. What are some ways we can worship God? We can sing praise songs to Him. We can play instruments. We also worship God when we tell other people about Him, when we read our Bible, and when we show God's love to other people. How is the boy worshipping God in the picture? *(he's singing praise songs to God with his guitar and reading his Bible)* **(I recommend reading all of Psalm 95 with your child. It's a beautiful description of God and lists several reasons why He is worthy of worship!)**

X is for anXiety

I Peter 5:7 NIV

•

Cast all your **anxiety** *on him*

because he cares for you.

Parent Help:

Anxiety. That's a big word! Have you heard of that word before? Do you know what it means to be anxious? Anxiety is just a big word for "worry" and "fear." What do you think the little girl in the picture is afraid of or anxious about? *(the dentist)* What are some things that scare you or make you worry? The word "cast" means to throw. Jesus tells us we can throw all our worries and fears on Him because He cares for us. And Jesus is big enough and strong enough to carry all our burdens and worries! So the next time you're worried *(anxious)* or fearful about something, stop and remember that Jesus loves and cares for us and He is more powerful than anything that scares us!

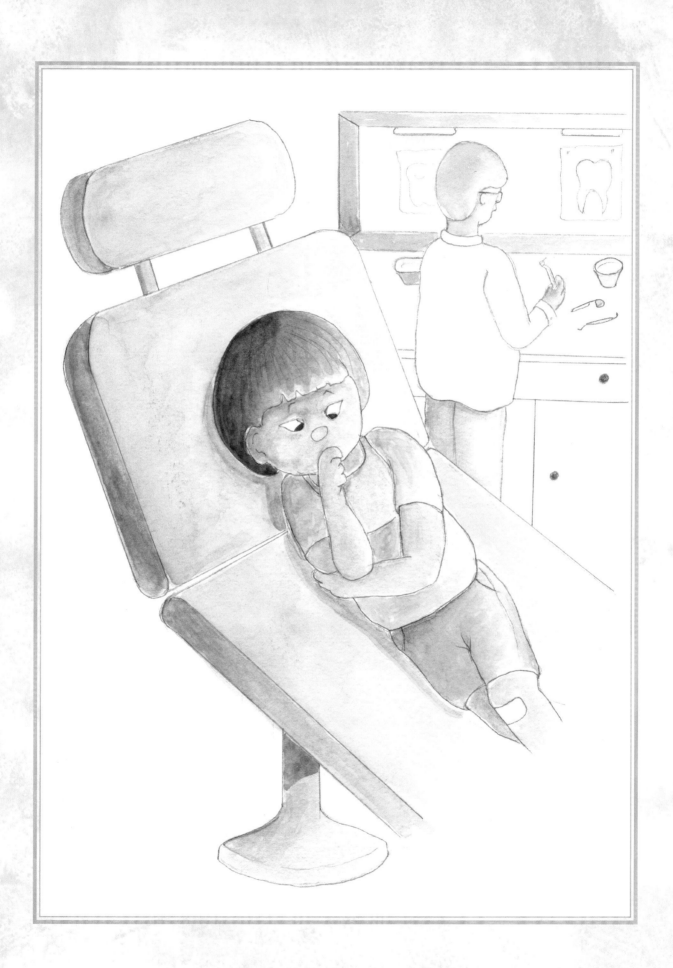

Y is for Your

Psalm 119:105 NIV

•

Your word is a lamp to my feet

and a light to my path.

Parent Help:

Whose Word is this verse talking about? *(God's Word)* What does God's Word do for us? *(It lights our path)* What do you use if it's dark outside to help you see? *(a flashlight)* A flashlight lights up the area in front of us so we can keep from stumbling when we walk. That's what God's Word does for us. It lights the way in front of us so we know where to walk. It guides us and directs us so we don't stumble and fall into sin.

Z is for Zealous

Revelation 3:19 NASB

·

Those whom I love, I reprove and discipline;

therefore be **zealous** *and repent.*

Zealous. Here's another big word you may not have heard of. Zealous means to be enthusiastic, eager, passionate. What are we to be zealous of? *(repenting)* What does repent mean? *(to admit you are wrong and turn from your sin)* Jesus says here that the ones He loves, He disciplines. Do your parents discipline you? They discipline you because they love you. Jesus also disciplines us because He loves us. He want us to be zealous....to be eager, quick and ready to repent, to admit we are wrong and turn from our sin.

Author's Dedication:

Dedicated to Elisa, Ashley, Daniel, Josiah, and Isaac. My motherhood dream was fulfilled when God gifted you to me.

About the Author:

It was through the AWANA program, first as a child, and later as a leader and commander, that Kimmie first became passionate about memorizing God's Word. When her children were toddlers and just learning to talk, she created her first "Verse Book" to instill God's Word on their hearts. Her favorite activities include meeting friends for coffee, discipling young women in the Word, and running with her dog Riley. Kimmie and her husband, Jim, live in North Carolina and have five children and one son-in-law.

Illustrator's Dedication:

For Karl, my husband, whose careful handling of Scripture has blessed my life incomparably.

About the Illustrator:

Jo has loved to paint and draw since the time her first grade art teacher asked if she could hang Jo's umimpressive, utterly simple painting of a tree on the wall of her little office. That was all the encouragement that little girl needed to pull the artist out of her. But her greatest love is her Lord Jesus and her greatest joy is sharing the hope that is found in His salvation. Jo and her husband, Karl, have four children and reside in Cary, North Carolina.